FLORIDA FAMILY LAW

SKILLS AND PRACTICE WORKBOOK

FLORIDA FAMILY LAW

SKILLS AND PRACTICE WORKBOOK

By

Ann Marie Cavazos

Associate Professor of Law
Director of the Legal Clinic & Pro Bono Program
Florida A& M University College of Law

Patricia A. Broussard

Associate Professor of Law
Florida A&M University College of Law

Nisé Nekheba

Associate Professor of Law
Florida A&M University College of Law

Nikie N. Lomax

Attorney
Young DeLoach, PLLC

Florida Family Law – Skills and Practice Workbook

Ann Marie Cavazos, Patricia A. Broussard, Nisé Nekheba & Nikie N. Lomax

Published by:

Vandeplas Publishing, LLC – January 2014

801 International Parkway, 5th Floor
Lake Mary, FL. 32746
USA

www.vandeplaspublishing.com

ISBN: 978-1-60042-213-3

ACKNOWLEDGEMENTS

All thanks be to God, my wonderful husband, John, and my children,

Ariel and Jerusha, for their love, support, and encouragement.

Ann Marie Cavazos

....

I am truly grateful for Robert Collins' indefatigable support

as my lifetime partner, best friend, and husband.

Nisé Guzmán Nekheba

....

I am ever so grateful to God for the love and support of my family,

especially my mom, Edith Lomax, and my grandmother, Johnie Lomax.

Nikie N. Lomax

....

Special thanks to the following persons for their invaluable input and guidance on this workbook.

PROFESSORS

Rebecca Olavarría,
Robert Minarcin,
Nicola Boothe-Perry,
Eunice Caussade-Garcia

ATTORNEYS

Jessica D. Thomas,
Camy B. Schwam-Wilcox,
Nathaniel Friends,
Shaz Asgha

REFERENCE LIBRARIAN

Lorelle Anderson

RESEARCH ASSISTANTS

Yang Liu,
Elizabeth Kathleen,
Betsy Daniller

Table of Contents

Preface

This Workbook is based on a fictional community of families who provide the scenarios for hypothetical exercises that are integral to the honing of practical legal skills. Users will become familiar with these families and their unique family challenges. In the Exercises, users will be required to perform real-life legal tasks for one or more families from this fictional community. The Workbook includes relevant statute(s), general case law, and internet links for the user who needs to act on or resolve Family Law issues. Each chapter also includes a checklist, though not exhaustive, of key interview questions to ask a client. Additionally, at the end of each chapter, the user is provided with a self-assessment tool which can be used to evaluate the user's performance on these tasks.

This Workbook may be used in a number of ways. The professor may assign chapters and exercises to be completed outside of class and direct students to use the checklist provided in each chapter as a tool for self-assessment. Alternatively, the professor may assign a chapter to be completed outside of class, collect the assignments, and assign a grade to the work product. This Workbook may also be used during class as a guide for in-class discussion and, depending on the class size, for in-class group assignments. This will allow for both self and group assessment, which supports the learning process and enhances skill building. This Workbook may also be used by individuals who plan to take the Florida Bar and wish to use it as a study guide. This Workbook is also designed to be used as a tool to assist new attorneys who plan to practice Family Law in Florida. It is also an excellent tool for paralegals.

With this Workbook, we attempt to fill a gap in the process of acquiring necessary skills to practice Family Law for Florida law schools, attorneys, paralegals, and anyone else interested in Florida Family Law. We hope that you will enjoy meeting the members of the fictional community, participating in the Exercises, and utilizing this Workbook in the manner that suits you best. We especially hope that this Workbook helps build better attorneys and equip them with the skills, confidence, and experience needed to serve the community with the highest level of professionalism.

Introduction to the Characters:

Real Housewives Of Loveville, Florida

Welcome to the town of Loveville, where the ladies are lovely and their relationships are tumultuous. This story will center on the lives of three women, as well as their families and friends, who live in the prestigious Lovely Lakes Subdivision.

The first is Maureen, mother of twin girls, Lillian and Julia, age ten. Maureen is married to Steve, who works as the CEO of his own construction company, Steve's Stonework, Inc. Steve started this company in June of 1992, one month after he and Maureen married. Maureen worked during the first nine years of their marriage, but they agreed she would be a stay-at-home mom once they discovered they were having twins. Maureen is the President of the Lovely Lakes Homeowners Association, which keeps her "in-the-know" about the ups and downs of the families in the community.

The second housewife is Kim, mother of three, Joshua, Corey and Kylah, ages eight, twelve, and sixteen, respectively. Kim is currently going through a nasty divorce with her husband, Chris, to whom she has been married for the past eighteen years. Chris moved out of the marital home a year ago and has been providing her with limited financial support since he left. The parties have accumulated substantial assets and debts during their marriage. For the first ten years of their marriage, Kim worked as an investment banker making at least $200,000.00 a year. After the birth of Joshua, Kim became a stay-at-home mom because Joshua is developmentally delayed due to injuries he sustained during child birth. The injuries cause him to experience severe seizures. Joshua has not spoken a word since he was born. Kim and Chris sued the doctor and the hospital for Joshua's injuries and won a huge settlement, which is currently held in trust. Since Chris moved out of the home, he has not been consistently sharing time with his children. He takes Corey overnight every other Saturday, but never takes Joshua. Kylah is not interested in spending time with her father because Chris is having an affair with Lisa, who graduated from her high school two years ago. Kylah has threatened to file for emancipation if she is forced to spend time with her father. Kylah has a part-time job working at a clothing retailer, Forever 21.

The third housewife is Tina, mother of none, wife of Tom. Tom is a successful venture capitalist and Tina is a prominent family law attorney. They have spent the bulk of their twenties and thirties building their nest-egg. Tina and Tom have tried desperately, but unsuccessfully, to conceive a child of their own. They have decided to pursue two new and different avenues to becoming parents. They are using a surrogate to carry their child. They are also going through an adoption agency to adopt a child in need of a loving home.

Samantha, Kim's sister, is Tina and Tom's surrogate, which is a convenient arrangement because Samantha lives in their neighborhood with her two children. Samantha is four-months pregnant with Tina and Tom's twin boys. Samantha has been divorced for two years. She has a permanent domestic violence injunction against her former husband, Jimmie, because he used to beat her and their children. A court has ordered Jimmie to pay child support and alimony but does not allow him to share time with his children due to his violent behavior. Jimmie has recently stopped paying child support and alimony because he feels that he should not have to pay support if he is not allowed to see his children.

Since it is important to Tina to be the best mother possible, she has decided to wind-down her family law practice so that she can focus on motherhood. Tina has several cases that she needs to resolve so that she can focus on her soon-to-be family. She has decided to refer her clients to you, along with any new referrals she receives. It will be your responsibility to meet with the clients and determine whether or not you can assist them with their legal issues. Many of the cases presented in the Exercises are from Tina's files. Please maintain confidentiality and be mindful of all other rules of professional responsibility.

AUTHORS' NOTES

AS A FAMILY LAW PRACTITIONER, THERE ARE A FEW AREAS OF INQUIRY YOU SHOULD ALWAYS ADDRESS WITH YOUR CLIENT.

If you are meeting the client for the first time, you should:

1. Conduct a conflicts check.

2. Ascertain that you have the client's correct and current contact information.

3. Explain the pertinent confidentiality rules and how they apply to the attorney/client relationship.

4. Explain that any advice you give is based on the facts presented by the client and, therefore, he or she should be honest and complete in relating them.

5. Ask if the client has spoken with or retained another attorney for the same matter.

6. Explain your fee in great detail and ask the client if he or she has any questions regarding the same.

7. Secure a retainer agreement from the client at the end of the consultation or as soon as practicably possible.

8. Once you have a signed retainer agreement, draft a client engagement letter detailing the scope of your employment, office policies, billing structure, and frequency of case updates or issues.

9. If the client has an existing court case relating to the matter for which he or she is seeking your assistance, ask the client to provide you with all pleadings and documents that he or she has on the matter. You should review the court file as soon as possible after being retained as counsel of record. If possible, review the court file prior to accepting the case to determine if the facts are as the client states them to be and whether there are any upcoming court appearances, filing deadlines, or pending motions.

NOTE TO STUDENTS AND NEW ATTORNEYS

What is a Self-Assessment Reflection and how does it apply to you, the student or new attorney? A Self-Assessment Reflection is composed of a self-assessment and a personal reflection. The Self-Assessment component is a means to evaluate or critique your abilities by highlighting the positive and negative progression of your legal analysis and the development of your critical thinking skills. It is an opportunity to evaluate and assess important areas of your skill-set based on your observation of your performance on the Exercises. The Reflection component serves to review your actions and determine whether those actions could be improved based on the knowledge gained from classroom discussion, the chapter checklists, case law, and relevant statutes. The Reflection component will build both your substantive knowledge and analytical skills, which will ultimately strengthen your lawyering skills. To ensure that you are using the latest materials available in this area of law, please be sure to periodically check the websites of Lexis-Nexis, WestlawNext, or your local law library for case law updates and supplements.

DISCLAIMER

While this Workbook is a fruitful introduction to family law in Florida, it is by no means a substitute for legal advice. The authors accept no liability for the contents of this book, or for the consequences of any actions taken on the basis of the information provided.

CHAPTER ONE

PREMARITAL AGREEMENTS

Exercise One

Lisa is dating Chris, who moved out of his marital home in Loveville, Florida, to live with Lisa in Cheatersville, Florida. Chris has been married to Kim for eighteen years. Three children were born during their marriage. Actually, Lisa babysat for Chris and Kim when she was younger, but did not establish a relationship with Chris until she turned eighteen. Lisa, who is now twenty years old, is set to inherit fifty million dollars when she turns twenty-one. Lisa is convinced that Chris is the love of her life and he has promised to marry her as soon as his very nasty divorce is finalized. Lisa is looking forward to becoming a stepmother to his children. Lisa's family has threatened to disinherit her unless she seeks legal advice from an attorney and has Chris sign an iron-clad marital agreement before she marries him.

Lisa has come to see you. Draft a list of issues and key points that you deem necessary to address in Lisa's agreement. In addition, draft a list of questions you need to ask her.

DO NOT TURN PAGE UNTIL COMPLETING THIS EXERCISE

Exercise Two

Hank is the heir to the largest soft drink distributor in North America. Hank loves Lola and desperately wants to marry her. Hank's cousin, Maureen, lives down the street from Lola in Loveville, Florida. Maureen is afraid that Lola will walk away with Hank's fortune if they were to marry and subsequently get divorced. Lola has a son by a previous relationship and is currently pregnant with twins fathered by Hank. Hank has come to see you for legal advice.

Draft a premarital agreement for Hank. What additional information, if any, do you need from Hank?

DO NOT TURN PAGE UNTIL COMPLETING THIS EXERCISE

Chapter Resources

RELEVANT STATUTE(S)

§ 61.079, Fla. Stat. (2013).

FORMS

Many of the forms you will need to practice family law in Florida can be accessed on the internet at:

http://www.flcourts.org/gen_public/family/forms_rules/index.shtml#900

FLORIDA FAMILY LAW RULES OF PROCEDURES

http://www.floridabar.org/TFB/TFBResources.nsf/Attachments/416879C4A88CBF04852 56B29004BFAF8/$FILE/311%20Family%20Law.pdf?OpenElement

A major part of your task is to select the correct form(s) to assist you in completing the Exercises.

CASES

1. *Francavilla v. Francavilla*, 969 So. 2d 522 (Fla. 4th DCA 2007).
2. *Macar v. Macar*, 803 So. 2d 707 (Fla. 2001).
3. *Widman v. Duggan*, 639 So. 2d 1071 (Fla. 4th DCA 1994).

Chapter Checklist

Did you ask or consider the following questions?

1. What are the full names, addresses, and birthdays of each party?
2. Has there been any duress or harassment with respect to the creation of this agreement?
3. When are the parties to be married?
4. What is the length of the period of time between the signing of the agreement and the wedding date?
5. What property is subject to the premarital agreement?
6. Are there any prior claims to property that is the subject of this agreement?
7. What provisions will be made for child support?
8. What provisions will be made for property acquired during the marriage?
9. How do the parties wish to dispose of their assets in the event either party dies during the course of the marriage?
10. Will the agreement affect the other party's right to inherit a portion of the probate estate?
11. Will the signing spouse be represented by counsel?
12. Was there complete financial disclosure by both parties?
13. Will there be provisions in the agreement in the event either party commits adultery?
14. Will there be provisions in the agreement regarding alimony?

SELF ASSESSMENT REFLECTION

WHAT I LIKED BEST ABOUT THE EXERCISE:

WHAT I LIKED LEAST ABOUT THE EXERCISE:

WHAT I LEARNED FROM THE EXERCISE:

SKILLS I HAVE ACQUIRED AFTER COMPLETING THE EXERCISE:

MY NOTES

CHAPTER TWO

ENTRY INTO MARRIAGE

Exercise One

Kylah's parents are going through a nasty divorce and she wants out of the house. She has decided to accept her boyfriend's marriage proposal and, along with him, has devised a plan to elope on the next full moon. Kylah is sixteen and her boyfriend, Matt, just turned fifteen. Kylah's friend told her that she read somewhere that you have to be a certain age in Florida to get married. She also said that the state allows a person to get married at a younger age if they have their parents' permission. Kylah is adamant about keeping her parents out of the loop. She has made an appointment to see you at your office and is in desperate need of counseling.

Draft a list of questions to ask her. What is your advice to Kylah?

DO NOT TURN PAGE UNTIL COMPLETING THIS EXERCISE

Exercise Two

Flora is twenty-two years old and madly in love with Herman. Herman has proposed and she has accepted and cannot wait for her wedding day. Flora has a secret that is keeping her awake at night and she does not know what to do. When Flora was fourteen, she had a mad high school crush on Tony. She truly believed that he was the love of her life and he felt the same. Their families were close and sometimes traveled together.

During one summer, when they were both fourteen, the families went camping in another state for a long weekend. Flora and Tony sneaked away for several hours and found a Justice of the Peace to marry them. (This state allows couples to marry at fourteen.) They never consummated the marriage because Tony's father received a job transfer before they could do so.

The family moved to Denmark and Flora and Tony kept in touch for a while, but eventually lost contact. Neither of them ever revealed their secret marriage and continued on with life as usual. Now, Flora is frantic and has come to you for advice. Her fiancé's religion prohibits him from marrying a divorcee.

What do you need to know about Herman and Flora's current circumstances? What are the legal issues? What advice will you give Flora?

DO NOT TURN PAGE UNTIL COMPLETING THIS EXERCISE

Rights within Marriage

Exercise One

Tom and Tina have been married for close to twenty years. They have no children, but are using a surrogate to start their family. Tom and Tina often take extravagant vacations all around the world. Last winter, Tina and Tom went to Aspen on a ski holiday. While there, Tom fell, hit his head, and was rendered unconscious for a few hours.

During that time period, he was rushed to the hospital to receive medical treatment. Tom's parents were also vacationing with them, so they went to the hospital with Tina. Once at the hospital, Tom's parents told Tina, that as Tom's parents, they should have control over his treatment. Tina was traumatized and felt she was being bullied. She told her in-laws that, as his wife, she could make final decisions regarding Tom's medical treatment.

Since then, Tom has fully recovered and is doing great. However, Tom's parents have stopped speaking to Tina because they believe she misread the law. They believe because Tom was birthed and raised by them and has known them far longer than Tina has, they should have had the final say in Tom's treatment. Tom has come to you and asked you to give him some legal talking points to convince his parents that Tina was correct and that they should not be offended.

What are the legal issues? What advice would you give Tom?

DO NOT TURN PAGE UNTIL COMPLETING THIS EXERCISE

Rights within Marriage

Exercise Two

Maureen and Steve are the parents of three lovely children. Steve has two other children, Josie and Jeb, from a previous marriage. Josie and Jeb are both in high school. Jeb is a bit of a firecracker and has been in trouble more than once.

In May, the principal called Maureen and Steve's house to say that Jeb would be suspended if a responsible adult did not immediately come to the school and discuss steps to be taken to change his behavior. Maureen immediately ran to the school, quickly handled the situation, and obtained a favorable outcome. Jeanie, Steve's first wife, and Jeb's mother is outraged. She believes that Maureen had no right to intervene in the matter.

In addition, Chris has been late three times in the last year on his child support payments. Jeanie has filed a complaint against Steve and Maureen asking the court to issue a garnishment order against their joint bank account. She is also seeking an order to bar Maureen from exerting parental rights over Josie and Jeb.

Maureen has come to you for advice. What legal advice can you give her regarding the two court orders she is seeking?

DO NOT TURN PAGE UNTIL COMPLETING THIS EXERCISE

Chapter Resources

RELEVANT STATUTE(S)

§ 741, Fla. Stat. (2013).

FORMS

Many of the forms you will need to practice family law in Florida can be accessed on the internet at:

http://www.flcourts.org/gen_public/family/forms_rules/index.shtml#900

FLORIDA FAMILY LAW RULES OF PROCEDURES

http://www.floridabar.org/TFB/TFBResources.nsf/Attachments/416879C4A88CBF04852
56B29004BFAF8/$FILE/311%20Family%20Law.pdf?OpenElement

A major part of your task is to select the correct form(s) to assist you in completing the Exercises.

CASES

1. *Hall v. Maal*, 32 So. 3d 682 (Fla. 1st DCA 2010).
2. *Beam v. State*, 1 So. 3d 331 (Fla. 5th DCA 2009).
3. *Anderson v. Anderson*, 577 So. 2d 658 (Fla. 1st DCA 1991).

Chapter Checklist

Did you ask or consider the following questions?

1. What are the full names, addresses, and birth dates of the parties seeking to marry?
2. Are both parties United States citizens with proper identification?
3. Is either party married currently married to another person?
4. Has either party previously been married? If so, was the marriage dissolved or annulled?
5. Have the parties taken a premarital education course?
6. Have the parties already entered or wish to enter into a premarital agreement?
7. Have the parties discussed issues related to having and raising children?
8. Does either party have children by a previous relationship?
9. What is the date of the intended marriage?
10. Have the parties acquired property during the marriage?
11. Is either party entitled to a pension or other monetary distribution?
12. Will the parties file a joint tax return?
13. Is either party a veteran?
14. What is the date of the intended marriage?

SELF ASSESSMENT REFLECTION

WHAT I LIKED BEST ABOUT THE EXERCISE:

WHAT I LIKED LEAST ABOUT THE EXERCISE:

WHAT I LEARNED FROM THE EXERCISE:

SKILLS I HAVE ACQUIRED AFTER COMPLETING THE EXERCISE:

MY NOTES

CHAPTER THREE

DOMESTIC VIOLENCE

Exercise One

While Kim and Chris continue their ongoing divorce battle, Chris decides to make an unannounced return to the marital home to remove some marital furnishings that he needs in order to make his new love den more comfortable for him and his girlfriend, Lisa. Lisa assists him in removing the items. Before Chris and Lisa could abscond with the furnishings, Kim and the children return home. Kim is furious. She tells the children to remain in the car, but Kylah, her sixteen year old daughter, refuses and goes into the house with her mother. A huge argument ensues, resulting in Chris pushing Kim against the wall and choking her. Kylah calls the police, but Lisa rips the phone cord from the wall before Kylah could tell the 911 operator what is happening. Lisa and Chris immediately leave the home after this incident. The police respond to the scene soon after the 911 call was disconnected.

What should Kim do? What are her rights in this situation? What should happen to Chris and Lisa? Explain both the civil and criminal implications of these events.

DO NOT TURN PAGE UNTIL COMPLETING THIS EXERCISE

Exercise Two

Kesha and John are living together, but are not married. Six months ago, Kesha gave birth to their baby girl, Aisha. This is John's first child and he adores Aisha. John believes he is the father, but recently caught Kesha in a compromising position with his cousin in their home. John is so enraged that he beat his cousin to the point of unconsciousness and then threatened to kill Kesha for being such a devious and scheming woman. Although he threatened Kesha, he did not hit her nor has he ever hit her in the past. John leaves the home and takes Aisha with him. Kesha then calls the police.

Kesha is panicked and comes to you for advice. How should she proceed? Explain both the civil and criminal implications of these events.

DO NOT TURN PAGE UNTIL COMPLETING THIS EXERCISE

Chapter Resources

RELEVANT STATUTE(S)

§ 741, Fla. Stat. (2013).

FORMS

Many of the forms you will need to practice family law in Florida can be accessed on the internet at:

http://www.flcourts.org/gen_public/family/forms_rules/index.shtml#900

FLORIDA FAMILY LAW RULES OF PROCEDURES

http://www.floridabar.org/TFB/TFBResources.nsf/Attachments/416879C4A88CBF04852 56B29004BFAF8/$FILE/311%20Family%20Law.pdf?OpenElement

A major part of your task is to select the correct form(s) to assist you in completing the Exercises.

CASES

1. *Oettmeier v. Oettmeier, 960 So. 2d 902 (Fla. 2d DCA 2007).*
2. *Bond v. Bond, 917 So. 2d 268 (Fla. 5th DCA 2005).*
3. *Doty v. State, 884 So. 2d 547 (Fla. 4th DCA 2004).*

Chapter Checklist

Did you ask or consider the following questions?

1. What are the full names and addresses of the parties? Have you included any aliases and nicknames?

2. What is the relationship between the parties (i.e. husband, ex-husband, girlfriend, neighbor, cousin)?

3. Do the parties live in the same household?

4. If married, have the parties separated? If so, when?

5. Do the parties have any children in common? If so, provide names and birth dates of the children.

6. Were there children present at the time of the incident? If so, is Department of Children and Families (DCF) involved?

7. What is each party's place of employment?

8. What is the physical description of each party?

9. When was the most recent incident of violence? Describe it in full.

10. During the most recent incident of violence, was anyone injured or threatened with bodily harm?

11. During the most recent incident of violence, were the police called? If so, were there any police reports, medical records, video recordings, or photos to show proof of injuries?

12. During the most recent incident of violence, were there any witnesses?

13. Are there prior incidents of domestic violence?

14. Are there any prior or current injunctions for protection against domestic violence currently in place against either party?

15. Does either party own, possess, or have access to a firearm?

16. Does either party have a history of violent behavior towards others?

17. Would you consider requesting a mental evaluation of the parents or children?

SELF ASSESSMENT REFLECTION

WHAT I LIKED BEST ABOUT THE EXERCISE:

WHAT I LIKED LEAST ABOUT THE EXERCISE:

WHAT I LEARNED FROM THE EXERCISE:

SKILLS I HAVE ACQUIRED AFTER COMPLETING THE EXERCISE:

MY NOTES

CHAPTER FOUR

PATERNITY

Exercise One

For the past year, Lisa, has been dating Chris, a local forty year old who has been going through a long drawn-out divorce. Lisa, a twenty year old aspiring Emergency Medical Technician (EMT), grew up in Lovely Lakes and recently enrolled in Loveville Community College's EMT program. At first, Lisa enjoyed Chris' attentiveness and romantic nature. Chris regularly sent Lisa her favorite flowers, Calla Lilies, and whisked her away to romantic weekend getaways to the Caribbean or to Le Chateau, a resort in Loveville's outskirts.

However, as time passed, and Chris's divorce proceedings lengthened, Lisa noticed Chris no longer had the energy or time to date her. Oftentimes, Chris preferred to stay at home or spend time with his son. Three months ago, Lisa decided to join a few of her girlfriends at La Nuit, Loveville's hottest nightclub. When Lisa and her friends entered the club, she was immediately hit by a tidal wave of sounds and senses that she had been missing -- the rhythmic, upbeat music; the symphony of liquor glasses with ice clinking, followed by rolls of laughter; and best of all, the unexpected attention from youthful, vibrant men her age.

That night, Lisa met Marco, a twenty-five year old personal trainer. Lisa and Marco immediately fell in love and began dating. A month later, transfixed by their intense connection, Lisa and Marco eloped and got married at the Loveville County Courthouse. In the meantime, Lisa never really broke up with Chris. She just stopped calling him or returning his calls. The newlyweds immediately rented a condo in the Lovely Lakes subdivision. They were very happy.

A few weeks later, Lisa ran into Chris at Loveville Community College. Chris was enrolled in a web design course. While still rooted in her own marital bliss, Lisa was struck by how sad Chris appeared and decided to catch up with him. Lisa and Chris sensed that they were still attracted to each other. That night, Lisa and Chris began to have an affair. Lisa became pregnant during this time. Despite this, Lisa decided to recommit to her marriage and stop dating Chris. Lisa never informed Marco about her affair with Chris. As a result, when Lisa gave birth to a healthy baby boy, Marco and Lisa were both elated. They both signed the baby's birth certificate and named the child Marco, Jr.

One day, while Lisa was pushing Marco, Jr. in his stroller at Lovely Lakes Bird Sanctuary, Chris happened to see them. Chris immediately approached Lisa and exclaimed, "You never told me you were pregnant! He looks just like me!" Lisa denied this and told Chris that her husband, Marco, was the baby's father.

Lisa and Marco insist that Marco, Jr. is their legitimate child because Marco Jr. was born while they were married. Chris disagrees. He wants to legally establish his parental rights and visitation with Marco, Jr.

Please advise Chris.

DO NOT TURN PAGE UNTIL COMPLETING THIS EXERCISE

Exercise Two

Mariaelena is Lisa's best friend. Mariaelena and Lisa have been friends since middle and high school, while attending The Excellence Academy (TEA), Loveville's exclusive prep school. They also spent summers together attending tennis camp. Mariaelena grew up in a very strict, yet loving family. Once she graduated from TEA, she decided to leave Loveville to attend a pre-med program at St. Augustine University, 100 miles away, to study neuroscience in its pre-med program.

During her sophomore year, Mariaelena met and began to date Kevin, a classmate in her organic chemistry class. Though they were happy together, Mariaelena broke up with Kevin because she noticed that Kevin was not as dedicated a student as she was. He preferred to party and smoke marijuana a few times a day. He was even arrested twice for possessing marijuana, with the intention to distribute it.

A few months after their breakup, Mariaelena discovered that she was pregnant. Feeling alone and in need of family support, Mariaelena took a leave of absence from St. Augustine University. She decided to return to her parents' home in Lovely Lakes until she gave birth to the child. Mariaelena's parents, Juana and Benjamin, were immediately supportive. Months later, Mariaelena gave birth to a beautiful and healthy baby girl, who she decided to name Marisol. Mariaelena never told Kevin that she was pregnant. She also never told her parents who was Marisol's father. Instead, Mariaelena signed the birth certificate and indicated that the father was unknown on the certificate.

Recently, Kevin found out about Marisol. Kevin is eager to assert his parental rights and legally establish custody as well as visitation. Mariaelena does not want Kevin to have any contact with Marisol, as she does not want her daughter exposed to Kevin's illicit habits. However, Mariaelena does want Kevin to pay child support.

Meanwhile, Mariaelena wants her parents, Juana and Benjamin, to legally establish their own rights to parent and jointly raise Marisol, while Mariaelena returns to St. Augustine to complete her pre-med studies.

Draft a client letter in which you advise Mariaelena.

DO NOT TURN PAGE UNTIL COMPLETING THIS EXERCISE

Disestablishment of Paternity

Exercise One

Lance, a twenty-six year old, recently returned to Loveville and reconnected with Amy, his high school sweetheart, who is twenty-four years old. Ten months later, Amy gave birth to Chelsea, at Loveville Children's Hospital. Lance presumed little Chelsea was his daughter and voluntarily gave Amy cash to support Chelsea's expenses. Two months after Chelsea was born, their relationship soured. Hoping that Lance would continue to financially support Chelsea, Amy drafted an affidavit for Lance to sign, in which he was to confirm that he is Chelsea's father. When Amy asked Lance to sign it, he refused. Lance had heard rumors about Amy dating James, while still dating Lance. He was no longer certain that Chelsea was his daughter.

Meanwhile, Amy continued to insist that Lance was Chelsea's father and that he should provide child support. Unbeknownst to Lance, Amy signed Lance's name on the affidavit and filed it at the local District Court. Amy then submitted a copy of this affidavit to Florida's Department of Revenue (DOR) with the intent to seek child support payments from Lance. The DOR contacted Lance and informed him that he was required to pay $500 a month in child support. Given Lance's doubts, he ignored this. In the meantime, Amy moved in with James.

Ten months later, Lance went to the DOR to assert that he was not Chelsea's father. Unfortunately, the staff member at the DOR showed Lance a copy of the affidavit that Amy submitted. Outraged, Lance yelled, "I never signed that! That's bogus!" The DOR staff member replied, "Well, you had sixty days to rescind your statement. But you never did."

Frustrated, Lance contacted the producers of the Lori Kovitch Show, Loveville's own popular TV show, where Lori often pitted lovers claiming or disclaiming paternity against each other to resolve the dispute. Touched by Lance's predicament, Lori decided to air Lance's case on her show. She invited both Amy and Lance to the show, as long as Lance and Chelsea were given DNA tests at Loveville Labs, Inc. a week prior to the show. Amy and Lance agreed. During the show, Amy and Lance shared their woeful plight with Lori.

At the end of the show, Lori waved a sealed yellow manila envelope in front of Amy and Lance. Lori dramatically ripped open the envelope, grabbed the enclosed report, and exclaimed: "Lance, you are . . . NOT Chelsea's father!" Lance immediately jumped up from his chair and yelled, "You see Amy! The truth, the absolute truth is setting me free!" Amy gasped, covered her face, and ran offstage; while the audience, now on their feet, clapped and roared.

Lance seeks your legal advice. He wants to legally disestablish paternity and stop the child support order. He also wonders if Amy can face criminal charges.

DO NOT TURN PAGE UNTIL COMPLETING THIS EXERCISE

Disestablishment of Paternity

Exercise Two

Meg and Ryan, both twenty years old and residents of Lovely Woods, a subdivision of Loveville, were dating for a month when Meg told Ryan that she was pregnant. While Ryan enjoyed dating Meg, he wasn't sure he was in love with her. However, given his traditional Loveville upbringing, Ryan wanted to act responsibly and asked Meg to marry him. Meg joyfully accepted and they were married in a small ceremony at the United Church of Loveville.

After the wedding, Meg moved into Ryan's small one bedroom condo in Lovely Woods. Several months later, Meg gave birth to a girl at Loveville Regional Medical Center. Meg and Ryan decided to name the child Sydney. For the next two years, Meg and Ryan made every effort to build a happy home together. Ryan worked long hours as an engineer at Tesla Utility Company, Loveville's largest utility company. Meg worked part-time as a per diem pediatric nurse at Loveville Children's Hospital. Meg's and Ryan's jobs gave them the flexibility to raise Sydney without sending her to day care by alternating their shifts.

Despite Meg and Ryan's efforts, the relationship became increasingly distant and strained. After three years of marriage, Meg and Ryan decided to get divorced amicably. They were each awarded equal time-sharing of Sydney, and Ryan agreed to pay monthly child support. Following the divorce, Ryan moved to a nearby condo in Lovely Woods, to stay near Sydney. Shortly afterwards, Meg and Sydney moved into her new boyfriend's home, which was also in Lovely Woods.

Years passed and Ryan continued to dutifully pay child support and visit Sydney. Meanwhile, Meg's boyfriend took an active role in raising and caring for Sydney. A few months ago, Meg's sister, April, called Ryan and told him, "I really admire how good you've been to Sydney, especially given that you're not the father." Although April assumed Ryan knew this, he did not, and was deeply shocked by this. Ryan immediately called Meg and confronted her about the news that April had shared. Meg denied this and reassured Ryan that he was definitely Sydney's father.

However, Ryan was no longer certain and became increasingly doubtful when he contacted other mutual friends who alluded to Amy dating Bob when she originally began dating Ryan. Although Ryan has grown to love and care for Sydney as his daughter, he is eager to find out the truth. After speaking with April, Ryan contacted Meg again and insisted that Sydney be given a DNA test to establish paternity. Meg refused her consent. Meanwhile, Sydney will turn eighteen years old in six months.

Ryan has come to your office to seek your legal advice. What advice would you give him?

DO NOT TURN PAGE UNTIL COMPLETING THIS EXERCISE

Chapter Resources

RELEVANT STATUTE(S)

§ 742, Fla. Stat. (2013).

FORMS

Many of the forms you will need to practice family law in Florida can be accessed on the internet at:

http://www.flcourts.org/gen_public/family/forms_rules/index.shtml#900

FLORIDA FAMILY LAW RULES OF PROCEDURES

http://www.floridabar.org/TFB/TFBResources.nsf/Attachments/416879C4A88CBF04852
56B29004BFAF8/$FILE/311%20Family%20Law.pdf?OpenElement

A major part of your task is to select the correct form(s) to assist you in completing the Exercises.

CASES

1. *Hooks v. Quaintance*, 71 So. 3d 908 (Fla. 1st DCA 2011).
2. *Mohorn v. Thomas*, 30 So. 3d 710 (Fla. 4th DCA 2010).
3. *Johnston v. Johnston*, 979 So. 2d 337 (Fla. 1st DCA 2008).
4. *Dep't of Revenue ex rel. Chambers v. Travis*, 971 So. 2d 157 (Fla. 1st DCA 2007).
5. *G.F.C. v. S.G.*, 686 So. 2d 1382 (Fla. 5th DCA1997).
6. *Dep't of Health & Rehabilitative Servs. v. Privette,* 617 So. 2d 305 (Fla. 1993).
7. *Dep't of Health & Rehabilitative Servs. v. Moore*, 603 So. 2d 13 (Fla. 5th DCA 1992).

Chapter Checklist

Did you ask or consider the following questions?

1. Was the child born out of wedlock?
2. Was the child from a voided or voidable marriage?
3. Was the child born during a valid marriage?
4. Has the father established a bond with the child?
5. What is the age of the child?
6. When did the issue of paternity arise?
7. Has petitioner acknowledged paternity after the discovery of his possible non-paternity?
8. Who can bring an action to establish paternity?
9. Who can bring an action to disestablish paternity?
10. Did the father ever legally assert or affirm that he was the child's legitimate father?
11. What steps are required to legally establish paternity?
12. What steps are required to legally disestablish paternity?
13. Is there a legal recourse if the mother refuses to permit the child to take a DNA test?
14. Are child support payments current or does a delinquency exists? If so, is there a reasonable explanation for the delinquency?
15. Has the client already attempted to resolve this matter through mediation?

SELF ASSESSMENT REFLECTION

WHAT I LIKED BEST ABOUT THE EXERCISE:

WHAT I LIKED LEAST ABOUT THE EXERCISE:

WHAT I LEARNED FROM THE EXERCISE:

SKILLS I HAVE ACQUIRED AFTER COMPLETING THE EXERCISE:

MY NOTES

CHAPTER FIVE

EXTENDED FAMILY CUSTODY AND GRANDPARENTAL VISITATION RIGHTS

Extended Family Custody

Exercise One

Janet, a beloved art teacher at Lovely Lakes Excellence Academy, recently died, while having dinner with her husband Jerry at the Talking Elephant. After an extensive autopsy, the Loveville medical examiner determined that Janet died from a high dose of arsenic poisoning. The official toxicology report concluded that Janet had been slowly poisoned with increasing doses of arsenic for the past four months.

After a detailed investigation by the Loveville Police and the Loveville Bureau of Investigations, detectives arrested Janet's husband, Jerry, and charged him with first degree murder. Jerry remains in prison awaiting trial, as he was unable to make the two-million dollar bail set by the Loveville County Judge. Meanwhile, Janet and Jerry have ten year old twin sons, Brandon and Fraser. Brandon and Fraser have been very distraught by losing their dear mother and being abruptly separated from their father. In an effort to care for the forlorn boys, Janet's only sibling, Xavier, immediately took Brandon and Fraser to his large Tudor-style home in Lovely Lakes, where he and his wife Tiffany could care for the traumatized boys.

However, upon hearing about Jerry's predicament, Jerry's sister Margaret flew to Loveville. Margaret lives in Cedar Hills, a large city a thousand miles west of Loveville. Jerry wants his sister Margaret to raise the twins until his unfortunate trial is resolved. Margaret is a successful veterinarian in Cedar Hills and is eager to take the boys away from this drama-filled case and the unwanted publicity. She knows it would be in the boys' best interest to leave Loveville and live in Cedar Hills until this matter is resolved.

Meanwhile, Xavier and Tiffany believe that the best balm for the boys' troubled souls would be to experience the least amount of change by continuing to live in Lovely Lakes, a community they've known all their lives, and by continuing to attend Lovely Lakes' Excellence Academy, alongside their closest friends. Xavier claims that the Excellence Academy offers a better education than the schools in Cedar Hills. He also claims that Margaret is not fit to care for the boys and has a history of abusing painkillers.

Janet and Xavier have come to your office for legal advice. They wish to seek permanent custody or, at the very least, temporary custody of the twins. How will you advise them?

DO NOT TURN PAGE UNTIL COMPLETING THIS EXERCISE

Extended Family Custody

Exercise Two

Layla, a thirty year old widow, has been living in a Lakewood cottage, a subdivision of Loveville, and raising her two children, ten year old Nina and six year old Sasha. Layla's husband, Dan, died unexpectedly five years ago while serving in the military in Iraq.

Since his death, Layla has worked tirelessly as executive chef at "The Talking Elephant," a successful Indian restaurant in a tiny part of Lovely Lakes, known for its succulent, unique dishes. Despite the palpable loss of a husband and father, Layla has worked hard to provide Nina and Sasha with a happy, healthy, and nurturing home. When Layla works long hours at the Talking Elephant, Layla's only sister, Mariah, has always been willing to baby-sit the girls and care for them.

Conscious of the girls' need for a good father figure, Mariah's husband Tory has been involved in attending the girls' volleyball and soccer matches. Tory has enjoyed supporting the girls' activities and achievements. A few weeks ago, while Layla was driving her girls to The Magic Forest, an amusement park near Loveville, they got into a serious car accident on the Loveville Parkway. Layla and the oldest girl, Nina, were seriously injured and airlifted to Loveville Regional Medical Center. Sasha was left unscathed.

Mariah and Tory rushed to the hospital. Layla is in a coma in the intensive care unit. Nina fractured her right hip and arm. Nina will need several surgeries and physical therapy. Layla's prognosis is unclear. The doctors informed Mariah that Layla may wake up and recover from her coma, or she may never emerge out of the coma. Nina is expected to make a full recovery.

Since the accident, Mariah and Tory have been taking care of Sasha in their own home in Lakewood, and visiting Layla and Nina regularly. The doctors have recommended that Nina should be transferred to Loveville Rehabilitation Center to begin intensive physical therapy.

Meanwhile, the new school year is about to begin in Loveville's public schools. Mariah has tried to enroll Sasha into Loveville Elementary School, but the school declined registering her because Mariah and Tory are not Sasha's legal parents. Furthermore, when Mariah tried to transfer Nina to Loveville Rehabilitation Center, the Center declined her request because Mariah is not Nina's legal parent.

Eager to ensure Nina's recovery and Sasha's enrollment in school, Mariah and Tory have come to your office to seek your legal advice. They would like to gain permanent custody or, at the very least, temporary custody of Nina and Sasha. What advice do you give them?

DO NOT TURN PAGE UNTIL COMPLETING THIS EXERCISE

Grandparental Visitation Rights

Exercise One

For ten years, Derek and Sharon seemed to be happily married, while living in the Lovely Lakes subdivision of Loveville. Derek and Sharon were certified accountants, and managed a thriving accounting firm. They have two children, Dallas, their eight year old son and Janice, their six year old daughter. Sadly, Derek suffered from major depression and recently committed suicide. Sharon and the children were devastated. While Sharon and the children were surrounded by thoughtful and supportive neighbors in Lovely Lakes, Derek's parents, Milly and Richard, immediately extended their love and support to Sharon and the children on a more regular basis.

Derek was Milly and Richard's only child. Through the years, Milly and Richard grew close to Sharon and their only grandchildren. They lived just a few miles away in Lovely Woods, a subdivision of Loveville. Soon after Derek's untimely death, Milly and Richard visited Sharon and their grandchildren several times a week, providing home-cooked meals, emotional support, and financial support.

While appreciative of her in-laws' love and assistance, Sharon begins to feel smothered by them. Additionally, her dear husband's unexpected death is causing her to yearn for a new beginning, a new home, and maybe even a new town and state. With this in mind, Sharon informs Milly and Richard she plans to move out of Loveville and that she would like to limit their visits. Sharon tells them, "You know that Dallas and Janice love you and that won't ever change. But we all need a fresh start to heal as a family, away from Loveville, and away from reminders of Derek. With that in mind, can you please only visit us every two to three months?"

Milly and Richard are hurt and shocked. Sharon's request threatens their understanding of family. Milly and Richard seek your legal advice. They would like to legally establish their parental and visitation rights as Dallas and Janice's grandparents. They would like their grandchildren to visit them every Sunday and during holidays.

Given the situation, do Milly and Richard have any rights to visitation? Draft a preliminary agreement for Milly and Richard.

DO NOT TURN PAGE UNTIL COMPLETING THIS EXERCISE

Grandparental Visitation Rights

Exercise Two

Mallory has had custody of her children, Michael and Monique, ever since her husband Mitchell was convicted of running a Ponzi scheme that fraudulently took the savings of several Lovely Lakes residents. Mitchell was convicted and sentenced to fifteen years in Lincoln Federal Penitentiary. In the aftermath of Mitchell's conviction, Mallory quickly divorced him and was awarded primary custody of their children. Their son Michael is seven years old and Monique is five years old. Once Mitchell was sentenced, Mallory moved away from Lovely Lakes with her two children because she could no longer face her Lovely Lakes neighbors' accusatory eyes.

With the loss of her husband's lucrative income, Mallory works long hours to support her family. She is the General Manager at the local Love-Mart Supercenter. While at work, Mallory has been able to rely on her sister Kelly's support. Mallory is also grateful to have her in-laws', Susan and Tyler's, support. Despite her divorce, Mallory welcomed Susan and Tyler's regular visits and time with the children, as it helped maintain a sense of normalcy and stability for the children.

Prior to the divorce, Mallory and the children grew close to Susan and Tyler, who lived nearby. The children grew up visiting their grandparents regularly and enjoyed going on fishing trips with them each summer. Mallory appreciated her in-laws' presence, especially since her own parents had passed away.

A few months ago, Mallory found out that Susan and Tyler became members of a small religious community that focused on prayer and prohibited the use of traditional medicine. While Mallory did not share these beliefs, she respected her in-laws' beliefs and thought it might serve to relieve them from the stress that Mitchell had caused in their own lives.

Lately, Mallory has become concerned by Susan and Tyler's increasing requests for their grandchildren to visit them. Susan and Tyler started insisting that Monique and Michael visit them on a weekly basis. A few days ago, Mallory took Michael and Monique to their pediatrician, Dr. Diane Ling, for their annual vaccinations. Monique surprised Mallory and the doctor when she refused to get vaccinated. Instead, Monique covered her arm and started kicking and screaming, "No! No shots for me. Grampy say it's a sin!"

Mallory was so upset that Dr. Ling was unable to vaccinate Monique. Mallory left the doctor's office confused, but planned to reschedule another appointment. That night, Mallory called Susan and Tyler and asked them why Monique refused to be vaccinated. Susan replied, "Well dear, our new religion is against it. It's a sin, plain and simple.

This new group has helped us regain our joy and peace. We've even enjoyed bringing Michael and Monique to services on Sundays." This was news to Mallory. While Mallory cared for Susan and Tyler, and respected their religious beliefs, she asked Susan to stop taking her children to their church. Mallory then decided that her children should only visit their grandparents one Saturday per month.

Since Susan and Tyler have a deep connection with Monique and Michael, Mallory's new request profoundly distressed them. In fact, given Mitchell's absence in the family, Susan and Tyler believe that it would be in the children's best interests to visit their paternal grandparents regularly — at least once a week, including an overnight stay. Mallory disagrees.

Susan and Tyler have come to you for advice. They would like to legally establish weekly visitations with their grandchildren, and an annual summer fishing trip with them as well. Will a court grant them visitation rights? What factors will the court consider in determining whether Susan and Tyler can have visitation with their grandchildren?

DO NOT TURN PAGE UNTIL COMPLETING THIS EXERCISE

Chapter Resources

RELEVANT STATUTE(S)

§751, (Fla. Stat. (2013).

§752, (Fla. Stat. (2013).

FORMS

Most of the forms you will need to practice family law in Florida can be accessed on the internet at:

http://www.flcourts.org/gen_public/family/forms_rules/index.shtml#900

FLORIDA FAMILY LAW RULES OF PROCEDURES

http://www.floridabar.org/TFB/TFBResources.nsf/Attachments/416879C4A88CBF04852 56B29004BFAF8/$FILE/311%20Family%20Law.pdf?OpenElement

A major part of your task is to select the correct form(s) to assist you in completing the Exercises.

CASES

1. *Mohorn v. Thomas*, 30 So. 3d 710 (Fla. 4th DCA 2010).
2. *Harrier v. Warmke*, 876 So. 2d 603 (Fla. 2d DCA 2004).
3. *Davis v. Weinbaum*, 843 So. 2d 290 (Fla. 5th DCA 2003).
4. *Brunetti v. Saul*, 724 So. 2d 142 (Fla. 4th DCA 1998).
5. *Beagle v. Beagle*, 678 So. 2d 1271 (Fla. 1996).

Chapter Checklist

Did you ask or consider the following questions?

1. Has one of the parents deserted the children?

2. Is the extended family member caring for the children on a full-time basis, and as a substitute parent?

3. Does the extended family member have the signed, notarized consent of the children's legal parents for the entry of an order of temporary or concurrent custody?

4. What are the legal names, dates of birth, and current addresses of the children?

5. What are the names and current addresses of the children's parents?

6. Where have the children lived for the past five years?

7. What is the extended family member's exact familial relationship to the children?

8. Is the extended family member receiving any financial support from the parent or the state?

9. Is there an imminent or pending Department of Children and Family (DCF) case?

10. Do the children have any contact with the parents?

11. Does the extended family member have any criminal background, history with alcohol or drug abuse, or history with mental problems?

12. How much contact or what kind of a bond does the extended family member have with the children?

13. What are the services or actions that the extended family member is unable to do without an order of custody?

14. Why is it in the best interest of the children to reside with or visit the extended family member regularly?

15. What is each child's preference in this matter?

16. Has another extended family member filed a similar cause of action?

17. What is the mental and physical health of each child?

18. What is the mental and physical health of the extended family member?

19. Has the client already attempted to resolve this matter through mediation?

20. Would you consider requesting a mental evaluation of the children and the extended family member?

SELF ASSESSMENT REFLECTION

WHAT I LIKED BEST ABOUT THE EXERCISE:

WHAT I LIKED LEAST ABOUT THE EXERCISE:

WHAT I LEARNED FROM THE EXERCISE:

SKILLS I HAVE ACQUIRED AFTER COMPLETING THE EXERCISE:

MY NOTES

CHAPTER SIX

GUARDIANSHIP AND CONSERVATORSHIP

Exercise One

Josie and Juan are well-respected members of the Lovely Lakes community. For the past ten years they have owned and managed JJ's Fiesta Creations, the region's most popular catering service. They have three children, Luna, Johnny, and Damaris, who are ten, eight, and five years old, respectively. A month ago, Loveville police and federal immigration officials stormed Josie and Juan's home and arrested them, claiming that Josie and Juan were undocumented and illegally residing in Loveville. The federal immigration court ruled against Josie and Juan, and ordered their immediate deportation. They were also legally barred from ever entering Loveville again.

Meanwhile, their children, Luna, Johnny, and Damaris were taken by Loveville's Department of Children and Family Services (DCF). The children were not deported because they were born in Loveville Regional Medical Center and are United States citizens. They have been shocked and traumatized by the abrupt removal of their parents from their lives. Juana, Josie's sister, also lives in Lovely Lakes with her husband Benjamin and their daughter, Marielena. She is distraught and fears that Josie's children will be separated, become wards of the state, and permanently be out of the family's loving reach.

Juana and her husband, Benjamin, are both United Sates citizens and are eager to raise Josie's children. For the past few years, they have worked as operating managers of JJ's Fiesta Creations and plan to continue to manage the entire operation in Josie's and Juan's absence. Juana and Benjamin have come to you to for advice on how to become the guardians of their niece and nephew.

Draft a set of questions to ask Juana and Benjamin. Draft a two-paragraph statement of advice for them.

DO NOT TURN PAGE UNTIL COMPLETING THIS EXERCISE

Exercise Two

Tom is sixty one years old and a long-time resident of Lovely Lakes. Tom suffers from a debilitating physical illness that has left him unable to care for himself. Although Tom is mentally competent, his rapidly deteriorating physical condition led him to petition the Loveville Court for a guardianship.

The court granted Tom's petition and appointed his son, Hugh, as his legal guardian. Tom and Hugh have always had a solid relationship. Their relationship continued to remain strong, until Hugh began dating Alicia, a high school teacher at the Excellence Academy in Loveville.

Tom has noticed that money from his retirement account at Loveville' Credit Union has been gradually decreasing. Recently, Tom also received a statement in the mail for a credit card he was completely unaware of, that was in his name. Tom believes that Hugh has been using his position as his guardian to take advantage of him and is afraid he may have credit liabilities he never agreed to and knows nothing about. Tom comes into your office desperate for legal advice as to what he should do to protect himself.

What questions would you ask? Explain the legal theories behind your questions and provide rules, defenses, and predict the likely outcome.

DO NOT TURN PAGE UNTIL COMPLETING THIS EXERCISE

Exercise Three

Tiffany has a thriving career as an artist in Loveville. She has made millions on her work. Over the years, she has had her ups and downs. Lately, Tiffany seems to be losing control. She has been seen walking the streets barefoot, driving with her daughter on the hood of her car, and even shaving her head.

Last week, Tiffany was found locked in Loveville Botanical Gardens' public bathroom. When the Loveville police went inside, they found Tiffany undressed and likely on drugs. The police transported her to Loveville Regional Hospital. The doctors have diagnosed Tiffany with schizophrenia. She is currently in the hospital's psychiatric ward, but will likely be discharged in seventy-two hours. Tiffany's family is concerned for her and her children.

What action can the family take? What will a court likely decide to do in this case? How will these events affect Tiffany's life and decision-making ability? Explain.

DO NOT TURN PAGE UNTIL COMPLETING THIS EXERCISE

Chapter Resources

RELEVANT STATUTE(S)

§ 744, Fla. Stat. (2013).

FORMS

Most of the forms you will need to practice family law in Florida can be accessed on the internet at:

http://www.flcourts.org/gen_public/family/forms_rules/index.shtml#900

FLORIDA FAMILY LAW RULES OF PROCEDURES

http://www.floridabar.org/TFB/TFBResources.nsf/Attachments/416879C4A88CBF04852 56B29004BFAF8/$FILE/311%20Family%20Law.pdf?OpenElement

A *major part of your task is to select the correct form(s) to assist you in completing the Exercises.*

CASES

1. *Rothman v. Rothman*, 93 So. 3d 1052 (Fla. 4th DCA 2012).
2. *Miller v. Goodell*, 958 So. 2d 952 (Fla. 4th DCA 2007).
3. *Leaird v. Leaird,* 540 So. 2d 243 (Fla. 4th DCA 1989).
4. *Vinson v. Sandusky,* 466 So. 2d 421 (Fla. 1st DCA 1985).

Chapter Checklist

Did you ask or consider the following questions?

1. Are all of the parties residents of Florida and over eighteen years old?

2. What is the legal name, date of birth, and current address for each minor or incapacitated person?

3. What is the relationship of the parties?

4. Have any of the parties ever been convicted of a felony?

5. Is the designee mentally and physically capable of being a guardian?

6. Can the children or the incapacitated person express their preference regarding this matter?

7. Has anyone else filed a similar cause of action regarding this matter?

8. What are the necessary legal steps required to remove or terminate a conservator or guardian?

SELF ASSESSMENT REFLECTION

WHAT I LIKED BEST ABOUT THE EXERCISE:

WHAT I LIKED LEAST ABOUT THE EXERCISE:

WHAT I LEARNED FROM THE EXERCISE:

SKILLS I HAVE ACQUIRED AFTER COMPLETING THE EXERCISE:

CHAPTER SEVEN

ADOPTION

Exercise One

Mary was a senior in high school when she met Harry. Harry was working at the local grocery store and planned one day to become manager and open up a store of his own. Mary was at the top of her class and was in line to become valedictorian. For Harry and Mary, it was love at first sight. They were inseparable from the moment they met.

Before graduation, Mary discovered she was pregnant. She was scared and ran to tell Harry the news. Harry comforted Mary and told her that everything would be okay, that he would take care of her and the baby forever. Mary was happy to hear that Harry was not going to leave her and quickly went home to tell her parents the news.

Mary's parents were very disappointed with Mary and told her if she planned on keeping the child she would have to move out of their home. Mary was only seventeen years old and had nowhere to go. Once again, she ran to Harry for comfort and support.

Mary went to Harry's parents' house and found that Harry had changed his mind. Harry told Mary that he didn't believe the child was his and was not going to take on such a responsibility. He also told Mary that he would not help her with the child or her pregnancy. Mary was devastated. She begged Harry to honor his earlier promise to her, but Harry did not budge. Harry told her it was best she go home, deal with her own problems, and leave him alone.

During her pregnancy, Harry did not support, communicate, or attempt to assist Mary in any way. Mary's parents did not change their position and demanded she be out of the house as soon as the baby was born if she planned on keeping the child. Mary felt she had no other choice but to contact an adoption agency and put up the child for adoption or risk being homeless. Prior to giving birth, Mary contacted and consulted with Best Place to Be Adoption Agency, (BPAA). They discussed her options and they agreed to place the child up for adoption.

Shortly before graduation, Mary went into labor and delivered the baby. The labor and delivery went well and there were no complications. After being discharged from the hospital, BPAA contacted Mary and scheduled a meeting to sign the required paperwork in order to proceed with the adoption.

Upon meeting with the representatives from the agency, Mary was clearly emotional about her situation. She was visibly upset and distraught. The BPAA representatives explained to her the conditions of the adoption and the ramifications of signing a voluntary consent to surrender her child. Mary signed the forms and the representative from the agency took the child from the hospital to be placed with the prospective adoptive parents.

The following day, Mary contacted BPAA and told them she had changed her mind. She explained that after coming home, Harry had changed his mind and wanted to marry her, be a family, and raise their child together. BPAA told Mary that there was nothing they could do and that they could not give the baby back to Mary.

Mary has come to your office and is desperate to get her baby back. What questions will you ask your client? Draft a letter explaining to Mary the relevant statutes and case law as well as the likely outcome of her claim.

DO NOT TURN PAGE UNTIL COMPLETING THIS EXERCISE

Exercise Two

Mary, the mother of a one year old child, has been recently arrested for prostitution. The Department of Children and Families (DCF) removed her child from the home and found the child to be malnourished and abused. DCF filed a dependency hearing in order to terminate Mary's parental rights. DCF argues it is in the best interest of the child to be placed with adoptive parents. DCF located an approved family eager to adopt the one year old.

DCF notified Bobby, the man who Mary claims to be the father, by sending him a letter informing him that they are seeking to terminate the mother's rights and proceed with the child's adoption. The letter notified Bobby that he had thirty-days to file a claim of paternity and an affidavit for commitment with the court. Both documents were required to preserve his rights.

Although Bobby and Mary were never married, Bobby was aware that it was possible that he was the father. Bobby at no time provided support for the child. After receiving the letter, Bobby tossed it into the trash. Upon her release from jail, Mary appeared before the court in her dependency hearing and consented to having her parental rights terminated. The next day, Mary and Bobby ran into each other in the street and it was love at second sight. They decided they want to keep their baby and be one happy family.

Draft a letter discussing the legal issues presented for both Mary and Bobby. Discuss the likely outcome.

DO NOT TURN PAGE UNTIL COMPLETING THIS EXERCISE

Chapter Resources

RELEVANT STATUTE(S)

§ 63, Fla. Stat. (2013).

FORMS

Many of the forms you will need to practice family law in Florida can be accessed on the internet at:

http://www.flcourts.org/gen_public/family/forms_rules/index.shtml#petsup

FLORIDA FAMILY LAW RULES OF PROCEDURES

http://www.floridabar.org/TFB/TFBResources.nsf/Attachments/416879C4A88CBF04852 56B29004BFAF8/$FILE/311%20Family%20Law.pdf?OpenElement

A major part of your task is to select the correct form(s) to assist you in completing the Exercises.

CASES

1. *Heart of Adoptions, Inc. v. J.A., 963 So. 2d 189 (Fla. 2007).*
2. *S.K.R. v. Dep't of Children & Family Servs. 902 So. 2d 328 (Fla. 2d DCA 2005).*
3. *T.R. v. Adoption Servs. Inc., 724 So. 2d 1235 (Fla. 4th DCA 1999).*
4. *In re Adoption of Doe, 543 So. 2d 741 (Fla. 1989).*
5. *In the Interest of I.B. J., 497 So. 2d 1265 (Fla. 5thDCA 1986).*

Chapter Checklist

Did you ask or consider the following questions?

1. Were there any signs of fraud or duress in the consent given by the mother?

2. Does a mother have the right to withdraw her consent to terminate her parental rights when the consent has not yet been entered by the court?

3. Can the unmarried biological father establish parental rights after he failed to respond to a properly served thirty day notice terminating his parental rights?

4. Was the father married to the mother at the time of the child's birth? If not, did the unmarried biological father acknowledge his paternity? If so, when and where did he acknowledge his paternity?

5. Did the unmarried biological father file a notarized claim of paternity form with the Florida Putative Father Registry?

6. Was the unmarried biological father identified to the adoption agency?

7. Did the adoption agency conduct a diligent search of the unmarried biological father of the child with the Putative Father Registry?

8. Was the unmarried biological father served with notice of intended adoption plan by the adoption agency?

9. Did the unmarried biological father file a claim of paternity with the registry within the thirty day notice period?

10. Upon service of the Notice of an Intended Adoption Proceeding, did the unmarried biological father execute and file an affidavit stating that he is fully able and willing to take responsibility for the child, setting forth a child care plan?

11. Did the unmarried biological father pay a reasonable and fair amount for the living and medical expenses incurred in connection with the mother's pregnancy and the child's birth?

12. Was the mother's consent for adoption given forty-eight hours after her delivery or the day she was notified she was fit for release from the hospital?

13. Was the mother's consent witnessed by two persons and acknowledged before a notary public?

14. Was the unmarried biological father provided with notice of the birth or adoption proceeding?

15. Is there a proceeding to terminate the unmarried biological father's parental rights pending adoption?

16. Did the unmarried biological father provide written consent prior to the termination of his parental rights pending adoption?

17. Did the unmarried biological father "demonstrate a timely and full commitment to the responsibility of parenthood?"

18. Did the unmarried biological father file a timely claim of paternity with the Putative Father Registry?

19. Does the Indian Child Welfare Act apply?

20. Was a home study done on the potential adoptive parents?

SELF ASSESSMENT REFLECTION

WHAT I LIKED BEST ABOUT THE EXERCISE:

WHAT I LIKED LEAST ABOUT THE EXERCISE:

WHAT I LEARNED FROM THE EXERCISE:

SKILLS I HAVE ACQUIRED AFTER COMPLETING THE EXERCISE:

MY NOTES

CHAPTER EIGHT

MINORS

Dependency

Exercise One

An Abuse Report was filed alleging DeDe Dunn (seventeen years old), and Linda and Mary Able (seven year old twins) were outside their house running around naked. When the Child Protection Investigator (CPI) arrived at the home, they found their mother, Mrs. Dunn-Able, outside naked "bathing" with the water hose. CPI and law enforcement attempted to convince Mrs. Dunn-Able to go in the house and put on some clothes but she became irate, turning the water hose on the CPI and law enforcement officers. Mrs. Dunn-Able was arrested and subsequently taken to a mental institution for medical observation and examination in accordance with the Baker Act.

The children said their mother required them to take a bath only twice per week. All "baths" were to be taken outside in front of the house using the garden hose and no soap. On investigation, it was determined that the bathtub in the only bathroom in the house was being used as a litter box for the twelve cats that lived in the house. The bathtub also did not have a working faucet. The house was found to be in disarray with cat feces scattered throughout. The children did not have beds and slept on the floor with the cats. The children were removed and sheltered. At the time of the removal, the mother's husband (and father of the twins), Mr. Able, was away in Indonesia obtaining "certification" to be a religious leader.

After a review of the parents' records, it was determined that the children were previously removed from the home approximately five years ago due to allegations of abuse and neglect. The mother has a history of drug use and mental illness. The children had been reunified with their parents approximately four years prior to the current removal.

When they were initially removed, the children were placed together in a foster home. Three months later, the foster home parents stated that the children were "too much" and requested that they be moved to another home. For the past four months, the children have been placed in two separate foster homes. DeDe is currently placed with the Goode family. Linda and Mary are currently placed with the Best family.

DeDe should be in the twelfth grade but, due to excessive absences from school, is currently in tenth grade and struggling with both Language Arts and Math. DeDe recently advised Mrs. Goode that she is eight weeks pregnant. Mrs. Goode has advised the agency that she is not willing to be a foster parent for an infant. She is willing to have DeDe stay at her home until the school year ends in June, but she would like to see DeDe placed somewhere else.

DeDe's father, Mr. Dunn, is currently incarcerated. He has not seen or spoken to DeDe in over four years. DeDe vehemently states that she is not interested in any relationship with her father. Last week, Mrs. Dunn-Able's parents contacted the case worker and advised that they have moved to the United States. They provided an address, and requested visitation with their grandchildren. When Mr. Able was advised of their request, he became very angry. He stated the grandparents do not like him and do not get along with their daughter. He further stated that Mrs. Dunn-Able would be extremely upset if she found out that her parents came anywhere near her children. The grandparents have clearly stated that if they are not allowed visitation with their grandchildren, they will retain the services of an attorney.

Draft a memo to your supervising attorney discussing the legal issues and predicting the likely outcome?

DO NOT TURN PAGE UNTIL COMPLETING THIS EXERCISE

Dependency

Exercise Two

Harriett is a single mother. She works two jobs in order to support her two minor children, Nicole, age twelve and Steven, age fourteen. They both attend Loveville Public Middle School and have repeatedly been told to come directly home after school. Harriett has told the children they are not to leave the house while she is at work and must be in bed by the time she gets home at night.

One night, after a long fourteen hour workday, Harriett came home to find food crumbs on the kitchen floor. Harriett grabbed the broom from the pantry and headed to the children's bedroom. Both children were asleep in their beds and Harriett turned on the light to wake them up. She asked them why there were crumbs on the kitchen floor. Before receiving a response, Harriet began to strike Nicole and Steven with the broom stick on their legs and buttocks.

The following morning, Nicole and Steven discovered bruises and welts on their bodies where they had been struck by Harriet. They both decided to tell a counselor at school what happened. The counselor called the Loveville Police Department. Harriett was arrested and charged with child abuse.

If you represent Harriett, what would be her best defense and the likely outcome? If you represent the children, as their guardian ad litem, what are the issues and what is the likely outcome?

Are there any ethical issues that might concern you as the attorney?

DO NOT TURN PAGE UNTIL COMPLETING THIS EXERCISE

Emancipation

Exercise One

Sarah is sixteen and lives with her boyfriend, John, in Love Creek, a sub-division of Loveville. She left her parents' house and started working to support herself. One night after work, Sarah got into a car accident and was rushed to Loveville Regional Medical Center. Sarah was unable to pay for her medical expenses. The hospital sent Sarah's parents the hospital bill and instructed them to submit payment. When Sarah's parents did not pay the hospital bill, the hospital filed suit to collect the balance.

Draft an outline delineating the hospital's best arguments? What is Sarah's parents' best defense? What is the likely outcome? Explain.

DO NOT TURN PAGE UNTIL COMPLETING THIS EXERCISE

Emancipation

Exercise Two

Laura is sixteen years old and just found out she is pregnant. Laura lives at home with her mother and six other siblings in Loveville. Laura's mother is absent a great deal and, when she is around, she is usually drinking. Laura and her boyfriend, Chad, want to start a life together. Laura wants to be emancipated so that she can get an apartment and open her own bank account to get ready for the baby. She contacts you and asks you for legal advice on becoming emancipated.

What advice do you give Laura? Draft a petition on her behalf.

DO NOT TURN PAGE UNTIL COMPLETING THIS EXERCISE

Chapter Resources

RELEVANT STATUTE(S)

§ 39, Fla. Stat. (2013).

§ 63, Fla. Stat. (2013).

§ 827, Fla. Stat. (2013).

§ 743, Fla. Stat. (2013).

FORMS

Many of the forms you will need to practice family law in Florida can be accessed on the internet at:

http://www.flcourts.org/gen_public/family/forms_rules/index.shtml#900

FLORIDA FAMILY LAW RULES OF PROCEDURES

http://www.floridabar.org/TFB/TFBResources.nsf/Attachments/416879C4A88CBF04852
56B29004BFAF8/$FILE/311%20Family%20Law.pdf?OpenElement

A major part of your task is to select the correct form(s) to assist you in completing the Exercises.

CASES

1. *Julius v. State,* 953 So. 2d 33 (Fla. 2d DCA 2007).
2. *King v. State*, 903 So. 2d 954 (Fla. 2d DCA 2005).
3. *Ison v. Fla. Sanitarium & Benevolent Ass'n*, 302 So. 2d 200 (Fla. 4th DCA 1974).
4. *Dora v. Cochran*, 138 So. 2d 508 (Fla.1962).

Chapter Checklist

Did you ask or consider the following questions?

1. If the children are removed from the home, what is the legal basis for their removal?

2. If the children are removed from the home, are they placed with families or in foster homes?

3. Are the children placed together or separately?

4. Are there alternative placements? If yes, did you conduct a background check and conduct a home study of prospective families for placement?

5. Is there a current case plan? If so, should it be modified? If yes, how would you go about modifying the case plan?

6. Should there be any contact between the children and their parents? If so, should it be supervised or unsupervised?

7. Should a guardian ad-litem be appointed or an attorney ad-litem? Should both be appointed? Why?

8. Should the children attend every court hearing?

9. If reunification is one of the goals, what steps would you consider?

10. Does the mother have to completely comply with the case plan?

11. If only the father complies with the case plan, will the children only be reunified with the father?

12. If parental rights are to be terminated, what must be done prior to finalizing the termination of parental rights?

13. Who should you contact prior to making a determination as to the goal for the children?

14. If any party is reluctant to meet or discuss the case with you, how should you handle it?

15. How would you go about finding out the medical status of the children?

16. Would you consider requesting a mental evaluation of the parents, children and the extended family member?

17. How would you go about finding out the educational status of the children?

18. Would you schedule visits with the children?

19. If emancipation is requested, how old is your client?

20. Does the parent know the minor's address?

21. Do both parents and the minor understand the consequences of emancipation?

22. Why does the minor feel it is in her best interest to be considered an adult?

23. How does the minor intend to support herself?

SELF ASSESSMENT REFLECTION

WHAT I LIKED BEST ABOUT THE EXERCISE:

WHAT I LIKED LEAST ABOUT THE EXERCISE:

WHAT I LEARNED FROM THE EXERCISE:

SKILLS I HAVE ACQUIRED AFTER COMPLETING THE EXERCISE:

MY NOTES

CHAPTER NINE

DISSOLUTION OF MARRIAGE

Exercise One

Mary married Ralph, on May 10, 2007, in Loveville, Florida, when they were twenty two and twenty four years old, respectively. Immediately following the marriage, they bought a condominium in downtown Loveville, and moved into it. In March 2008, Mary gave birth to twins, Steven and Linda.

Throughout the marriage, Mary and Ralph have argued about finances and Ralph's extra-marital affairs. For the past five years, Ralph has worked as an Operations Manager at Loveville Botanical Gardens, earning $60,000 a year, while Mary has been a nurse at Loveville Regional Hospital, earning $55,000 a year. In December 2012, Mary moved out of their condo and took the twins with her. Ralph has desperately looked for them but to no avail. He believes Mary moved back to Boston with their children.

Ralph has come to you to seek your legal advice. Ralph wants the full value of the house, joint custody of the twins, child support, and alimony.

Draft a letter to Ralph outlining his rights and responsibilities to Mary and their children. Advise him as to what property he is entitled to in the divorce settlement.

DO NOT TURN PAGE UNTIL COMPLETING THIS EXERCISE

Exercise Two

Nicole married Andy on January 1, 2001, in Loveville, Florida, when they were twenty-five and twenty-seven years old, respectively. Upon Nicole's suggestion, they purchased a condominium in downtown Loveville, and moved into it. In March of 2003, Nicole gave birth to twins, Madison and Morgan. Prior to the twins' birth, Nicole worked as a registered nurse, while Andy worked as CEO of Loveville Distribution, Inc. However, once the twins were born, Nicole yearned to work at home raising the twins, with the plan to return to the nursing field in a year or two. Meanwhile, Andy left Loveville Distribution, Inc. and established his own distribution company.

Oftentimes, Nicole spent a few hours a week assisting Andy's business by attending conferences, networking, and obtaining new clients. Andy's business became very successful. In 2012, the company's gross revenue was $750,000.00. In 2010, Nicole and Andy sold their condo, and purchased a single-family home in Loveville. In 2011, Andy purchased a vacation home in Puerto Rico. The title to the vacation home is solely in Andy's name.

Throughout the marriage, Nicole and Andy have argued about finances and Nicole's extra-marital affairs. By 2009, Nicole wanted to return to the nursing field, but Andy wanted her to remain at home raising the twins. In June 2012, Nicole kicked Andy out of their home and changed the locks. Since then, Andy has been living with a relative in Kissimmee, Florida.

Since she kicked him out of their home, Nicole has not allowed Andy to visit the twins. Nicole has also filed a restraining order against Andy, claiming that he has threatened her. Andy denies this. Andy does admit that, since being kicked out, he secretly visits their property every Saturday to get a glimpse of his children without actually entering the home. At times, he has even climbed trees on the property to take pictures of his children, who he misses desperately. Nicole caught him doing this a few times, was spooked, and called the Loveville Police Department.

Nicole wants a divorce and has sought your advice. She wants the full value of the house, sole parental responsibility of the twins, child support, and alimony. She also wants Andy to pay for her medical school expenses.

Draft a sample petition for dissolution of marriage for Nicole based on the law and advise her on the likelihood of the court awarding her sole parental responsibility.

DO NOT TURN PAGE UNTIL COMPLETING THIS EXERCISE

Equitable Distribution

Exercise One

Mary married Ralph on May 10, 2001, in Loveville, Florida, when they were twenty-five and twenty-seven years old, respectively. Immediately following the marriage, they purchased and moved into a condominium in downtown Loveville. In March of 2003, Mary gave birth to twins, Steven and Linda. Prior to getting married, Mary was a paralegal, while Ralph was an Operations Manager at Gator World. Once the twins were born, Mary became a full-time homemaker, with plans to return to the legal field or go to law school in a year or two. Meanwhile, Ralph left Gator World, and established his own event planning business. Oftentimes, Mary spent a few hours a week assisting Ralph's business by attending conferences, networking, and obtaining new clients. Ralph's business became very successful. In 2012, the gross revenue from his business was $750,000.00.

In 2010, Ralph and Mary sold their Orlando condo, and purchased a home in Windermere, Florida. In 2011, Ralph purchased a vacation home in Puerto Rico, with only his name on the deed. Throughout the marriage, Mary and Ralph have argued about finances and Mary's extra-marital affairs. By 2009, Mary wanted to return to the legal field, but Ralph wanted her to remain at home to raise the twins.

In June 2012, Mary kicked Ralph out of their home and changed the locks. Since then, Ralph has been living with a relative in Kissimmee, Florida. Since she kicked him out of their home, Mary has not allowed Ralph to visit the twins. Mary also filed a restraining order against Ralph, claiming that he threatened to kill her. Ralph denies this. Ralph admits that since being kicked out, he secretly visits their property every Saturday to get a glimpse of the children without actually entering the home. At times, he has even climbed trees on the property to take pictures of his children, whom he misses desperately. Mary caught him doing this a few times, was spooked, and called the Windermere Police Department.

Ralph wants a divorce, the full value of the house, equal time-sharing of the twins, and child support. Mary wants the full value of the house, sole custody of the twins, child support, alimony, and for Ralph to pay for Mary to go to law school. Ralph has come to you to seek your legal advice.

Draft a memo explaining equitable distribution to him and outlining what property he would be entitled to retain once the divorce becomes final.

DO NOT TURN PAGE UNTIL COMPLETING THIS EXERCISE

Equitable Distribution

Exercise Two

Mary legally married Rachel on May 10, 2011, in Boston, Massachusetts. Immediately following the marriage, Mary inherited a house from her parents in Ocala, Florida. The couple and their adopted infant, Steven, moved into the home. The house was in disrepair. Rachel made substantial repairs to the house with money from her life savings that raised the property value and brought rave reviews from the neighbors on the landscaping and decor.

Rachel, a former officer in the military, has a comfortable pension from the government, which is direct deposited into their joint bank account every month. Throughout the marriage, Mary and Rachel have argued about finances. In December 2012, the relationship had become so strained that Mary left Rachel and moved to Loveville, Florida, with their son Steven. Mary wants a fresh start and a quick divorce. Mary wants sole custody of Steven, child support, and the entire value of their home in Ocala, Florida.

Mary has come to you to seek your legal advice on what she and Steven will be entitled to receive from Rachel. Draft a client letter explaining the legal advice and predicting the likely outcome?

DO NOT TURN PAGE UNTIL COMPLETING THIS EXERCISE

Alimony

Exercise One

Fred and Martha are good friends of Tina and Tom. Fred has some questions about getting a divorce, but does not wish to talk to Tina, an attorney; for fear that it may cause a conflict between friends when all he wants is advice.

Fred and Martha have been married for fifteen years. Martha is a very successful doctor at Loveville Regional Hospital and makes a seven figure salary. Fred and Martha had a huge argument; one of the biggest they have ever had. Because of some of the nasty things that were said, Fred is exploring his options, which include a possible divorce.

Fred supported Martha through medical school and her residency. In addition, during this time period, Fred took care of Martha's mother who was gravely ill and living with them. Fred wants to know if, in the event of a divorce, he would be entitled to alimony. If he is entitled to alimony, he would like to know the type and the amount of the alimony he would receive. He also wants to know if he can get a lump sum based on the value of Martha's medical license.

Draft a client letter outlining Fred's rights under the facts he has given you.

DO NOT TURN PAGE UNTIL COMPLETING THIS EXERCISE

Alimony

Exercise Two

Mary married Ralph, on May 10, 2009, in Loveville, Florida, when they were eighteen and twenty-one years old, respectively. Immediately following the marriage, they began renting a condo in downtown Loveville. Mary is a student at the University of Central Florida. Ralph works odd jobs here and there, but has never held down a steady job.

Throughout the marriage, Mary and Ralph argued about finances and Ralph's constant cocaine use. In January 2010, their son Steven was born. In January 2012, Mary and Ralph started sleeping in separate bedrooms in their condo. The relationship has become so strained that Mary wants a fresh, healthier start for her and Steven. Because Ralph is always high on cocaine, Mary believes he is an unfit parent who cannot keep a steady job or care for Steven.

Mary wants a divorce, alimony, child support, and sole custody of Steven, with no visitation rights for Ralph. She is concerned about her rights to alimony and has come to you to seek your legal advice on that particular topic.

What advice would you give Mary and what further information do you need?

DO NOT TURN PAGE UNTIL COMPLETING THIS EXERCISE

Chapter Resources

RELEVANT STATUTE(S)

§ 61, Fla. Stat. (2013).

FORMS

Many of the forms you will need to practice family law in Florida can be accessed on the internet at:

http://www.flcourts.org/gen_public/family/forms_rules/index.shtml#900

FLORIDA FAMILY LAW RULES OF PROCEDURES

http://www.floridabar.org/TFB/TFBResources.nsf/Attachments/416879C4A88CBF04852
56B29004BFAF8/$FILE/311%20Family%20Law.pdf?OpenElement

A major part of your task is to select the correct form(s) to assist you in completing the Exercises.

CASES

1. *Levy v. Levy*, 862 So. 2d 48 (Fla. 3d DCA 2003).
2. *Kazmierazak v. Query*, 736 So. 2d 106 (Fla. 4th DCA 1999).
3. *Rosen v. Rosen,* 696 So. 2d 697 (Fla. 1997).
4. *Freeman v. Freeman*, 468 So. 2d 326 (Fla. 5th DCA 1985).

Chapter Checklist

Did you ask or consider the following questions?

1. What are the full names and addresses of the parties?
2. Was a conflict check done?
3. When and where were the parties married?
4. Have the parties separated? If so, when?
5. Is either party on active duty with the military?
6. Can the marriage be reconciled through counseling or is the marriage irretrievably broken?
7. Do the parties have any dependent or minor children in common that were born prior to or during the marriage? What are the ages of the children?
8. What is the educational background of each party?
9. Are the parties employed? If so, what are their incomes?
10. Is either party disabled or unable to work?
11. Is either party mentally incapacitated?
12. Has either party forgone career advancement to be the homemaker or to advance the career of the other spouse?
13. What assets were acquired during the marriage? What assets were acquired prior to the marriage? What are the marital debts?
14. Is either party seeking alimony?
15. Were any assets inherited?
16. Was there any domestic violence during the marriage?
17. Was either party ever abusive towards the children?
18. Do the parties have a premarital agreement?
19. Does the wife want to restore her maiden name? If so, does she qualify?
20. Who was the primary caregiver of the children during the marriage?
21. Does either party have a substance abuse problem?
22. Should a guardian ad-litem be hired or appointed?
23. What are the terms of your client's proposed parenting plan?
24. Will this be a contested or an uncontested divorce?
25. Have the parties attempted mediation?

SELF ASSESSMENT REFLECTION

WHAT I LIKED BEST ABOUT THE EXERCISE:

WHAT I LIKED LEAST ABOUT THE EXERCISE:

WHAT I LEARNED FROM THE EXERCISE:

SKILLS I HAVE ACQUIRED AFTER COMPLETING THE EXERCISE:

MY NOTES

CHAPTER TEN

PARENTAL RESPONSIBILITY, TIME-SHARING AND CHILD SUPPORT

Exercise One

Kim and Chris are the parents of three children: Kylah, Corey, and Joshua; ages sixteen, twelve and eight, respectively. At birth, Joshua suffered injuries that caused him to be developmentally delayed. The injuries cause him to experience severe seizures. Joshua has not spoken a word since he was born. Because of Joshua's disabilities, Kim has been a stay-at-home mother since his birth. Kim and Chris filed for divorce a year ago. The children reside with Kim.

Since filing for divorce, Chris provides Kim with limited financial support. Recently, Chris decided to move to Australia and, once he relocates, wants the children to visit him five times a year, at least. He does not want to pay child support since he will be paying the travel costs associated with having the children visit him. He also wants to have a say in the children's day-to-day affairs after he moves to Australia. Since Chris moved out of the family home, he has not been sharing the child rearing responsibilities equally with Kim.

Corey stays with him overnight every other Saturday, but Joshua never does. Instead, Joshua always stays with Kim. Kylah does not spend any time with Chris either. Kylah is not interested in spending time with Chris because he is having an affair with Lisa, who graduated from her high school two years ago. Kylah has threatened to file for emancipation if she is forced to spend time with her father.

Kim has come to you for advice. What are her rights in this situation? Will Chris have to pay child support? Will the court award Kim sole parental responsibility once Chris moves to Australia?

DO NOT TURN PAGE UNTIL COMPLETING THIS EXERCISE

Exercise Two

Blake and Carrie were married on May 10, 2007, in Loveville, Florida. They have two children born during the marriage, Missy and Tony, who are eighteen months apart in age. Blake and Carrie love wine and both are known to consume large quantities as members of Loveville's Wine Tasting Club.

In January 2012, Blake and Carrie started sleeping in separate bedrooms in their home. Most of the time, Carrie sleeps in Missy's bedroom while Blake sleeps in the master bedroom. The marital relationship has become strained and Carrie wants a fresh, healthier start for both her and the children.

Carrie believes that Blake is an unfit parent who consumes large quantities of wine. She has secretly photographed Blake drinking at wine tasting events and is convinced that he is an alcoholic even though they have been known to consume the same amount of wine. Carrie claims that the fact that Blake cannot keep a steady job is proof of his alcoholism. She wants a divorce and has insisted that Blake have no visitation rights.

Carrie has come to see you. What advice would you give her?

DO NOT TURN PAGE UNTIL COMPLETING THIS EXERCISE

Exercise Three

Kim and Chris have three children: Kylah, Corey and Joshua; ages sixteen, twelve, and eighteen, respectively. Kim is currently going through a nasty divorce with Chris, to whom she has been married for the past eighteen years. Chris moved out of state, but wants to have maximum contact with his children. All three children are in public schools near the home they share with their mother in Loveville.

In addition, all of the children are involved in extra-curricular activities, which their psychologist claims helps them take their minds off of the divorce. Kylah is a level eight competitive gymnast. She is in the gym six days a week from 3:00 p.m. to 9:00 p.m., Mondays through Fridays and on Saturdays from 9 a.m. to 1:00 p.m. Corey loves music and he is a member of his school band. He also studies voice and piano three to four days a week after school. Joshua is on the football and basketball team and will soon graduate.

Chris has retained you to draft a parenting plan that includes a time-sharing schedule. Chris wants you to draft a plan that will be fair to all parties involved.

DO NOT TURN PAGE UNTIL COMPLETING THIS EXERCISE

Exercise Four

Fred and Martha have twins, Fred, Jr. and Christy. They both reside in Loveville, Florida, and were never married to each other. Fred is a serious and dedicated parent who believes in honoring his financial and emotional obligations to his children. Fred had been enjoying frequent and liberal visits with the children until two months ago, when Martha found out that Fred recently became engaged. Since then, Martha has refused to allow Fred to see the children. Fred is distraught and comes to you for assistance.

What are Fred's rights and what can be done to fix this problem?

DO NOT TURN PAGE UNTIL COMPLETING THIS EXERCISE

Exercise Five

Jerry and Kate have been sweethearts since they were in the third grade. They always thought they would get married and raise a big family in Loveville. Jerry joined the military to earn money for them to start their wonderful future together. He was deployed to Iraq in February 2005.

Shortly after arriving there, Kate contacted him to say she was pregnant. Kate gave birth to a girl, whom they named Kelly. Jerry was delighted about the birth of their daughter and, as soon as he returned to Loveville, he and Kate were married. Afterwards, Jerry and Kate had two more children. Unfortunately, the marriage did not last and they divorced. All three children live with Kate. Jerry pays $800.00 a month in child support. In addition, he pays for Kelly's dance lessons, gymnastics, and orthodontia.

While at "Talk of the Town," a bar in downtown Loveville, Jerry ran into a high school buddy, Fred, whom he had not seen in years. As they talked about old times, Fred asked Jerry if he ever heard from that girl, "Kate," that he once dated. Fred revealed that his older brother, Jack, had a daughter named Kelly with Kate. Fred added that Jack is a good father who has given Kate $600.00 a month in child support for Kelly and had done so since her birth, even though Jack now lives in Spain. Fred told Jerry that Jack also pays for Kelly's gymnastics, dance lessons, and her orthodontia.

Jerry confronted Kate, who confessed that Jerry is not Kelly's father and that she has been receiving money from Jack for years. Blood tests have revealed that Jerry is the father of the other two children. Jerry does not want Kate to be charged with any type of criminal or fraud actions, but he does want her to reimburse him for the child support and lessons he has paid for Kelly.

Jerry has come to your office. Please advise him.

DO NOT TURN PAGE UNTIL COMPLETING THIS EXERCISE

Exercise Six

Kesha and Tony lived together for five years, but broke up one year ago due to Tony's infidelity. They have two children in common, Morgan and Madison, three year old twins, born out of wedlock. Tony works full-time at a major engineering firm and makes approximately $80, 0000.00 a year. Kesha works part-time at the public library and goes to school full-time. Kesha makes about $20,000.00 a year. Since the break-up, Kesha has struggled to make ends meet. In order to have enough money to cover all of her bills, Kesha applied for public assistance.

In keeping with their policy, the Florida Department of Revenue (DOR) required Kesha to pursue Tony for child support. Kesha did not inform the DOR that Tony had been giving her $800.00 a month to meet the financial needs of the children or that he provided them with financial support the entire time they lived together. Tony was subsequently served with a petition for child support from the DOR on behalf of Kesha seeking ongoing child support and two years of retroactive support for the children.

Tony has come to you for assistance in resolving the child support issue and getting his rights established, so he can share time with the children. Please advise him on his rights and how you will proceed in this matter.

DO NOT TURN PAGE UNTIL COMPLETING THIS EXERCISE

Chapter Resources

RELEVANT STATUTE(S)

§ 61, Fla. Stat. (2013).

§ 409, Fla. Stat. (2013).

§ 741, Fla. Stat. (2013).

§ 742, Fla. Stat. (2013).

FORMS

Many of the forms you will need to practice family law in Florida can be accessed on the internet at:
http://www.flcourts.org/gen_public/family/forms_rules/index.shtml#900

FLORIDA FAMILY LAW RULES OF PROCEDURES

http://www.floridabar.org/TFB/TFBResources.nsf/Attachments/416879C4A88CBF04852 56B29004BFAF8/$FILE/311%20Family%20Law.pdf?OpenElement

A major part of your task is to select the correct form(s) to assist you in completing the Exercises.

CASES

1. *Lane v. Lane, 16 So. 3d 179 (Fla. 5th DCA 2009).*
2. *Washington v. Stevens, 969 So. 2d 487 (Fla. 5th DCA 2007).*
3. *Cheverie v. Cheverie, 898 So. 2d 1028 (Fla. 5th DCA 2005).*
4. *Levy v. Levy, 862 So. 2d 48 (Fla. 3d DCA 2003).*
5. *Kazmierazak v. Query, 736 So. 2d 106 (Fla. 4th DCA 1999).*

Chapter Checklist

Did you ask or consider the following questions?

1. What are the names, ages, and birth dates of the minor children of the marriage?

2. Have the parties created a parenting plan or entered into an informal time-sharing or child support agreement?

3. Where do the parties currently reside and with whom do the children currently reside?

4. How far apart are the residences of the parties?

5. Have the children expressed a preference for which parent they wish to reside with on a permanent basis?

6. Does either parent suffer from mental illness or an addiction?

7. Does either parent plan to move out of state or more than 50 miles from their current residence? What are the occupations and incomes of the parties?

8. Does either party pay for health insurance, dental insurance, or child care for the minor children? If so, what are the costs?

9. Which party is most likely to facilitate an ongoing relationship between the other party and the children?

10. Has either party ever refused to allow the children to spend time with the other parent?

11. Would contact with either parent be detrimental to the physical, emotional, or mental well-being of the children?

12. Has either party been abusive towards the children?

13. Do you understand what is meant by equal time-sharing?

14. Do you understand what is meant by sole parental responsibility?

15. Should a guardian ad-litem be hired or appointed by the court?

SELF ASSESSMENT REFLECTION

WHAT I LIKED BEST ABOUT THE EXERCISE:

WHAT I LIKED LEAST ABOUT THE EXERCISE:

WHAT I LEARNED FROM THE EXERCISE:

SKILLS I HAVE ACQUIRED AFTER COMPLETING THE EXERCISE:

MY NOTES

CHAPTER ELEVEN

MODIFICATION OF ORDERS

Exercise One

Jerry and Kate have been sweethearts since they were in the third grade. They always thought that they would get married and raise a big family in Loveville. Jerry joined the military to earn money for them to start their wonderful future together. He was deployed to Iraq in February 1994. Shortly after arriving there, Kate contacted him to say she was pregnant. Kate gave birth to a girl, whom they named Kelly. Jerry was delighted and as soon as he returned to Loveville, they were married. Afterwards, Jerry and Kate had two more children.

Unfortunately, the marriage did not last and they divorced in 2004. The children live with Kate. Jerry pays $800.00 a month in child support. In addition, Jerry pays for Kelly's dance lessons, gymnastics, and orthodontia. In 2009, when Jerry learned that he was not Kelly's biological father, he filed a petition to disestablish paternity. The court ordered Jerry to continue to pay child support to Kate for Kelly. Jerry is bitter about having to pay child support for a child that is not his. He wants the court to modify the child support order.

Will Jerry be allowed to have the child support order modified? If so, draft a motion to modify the amount of child support Jerry currently pays Kate for Kelly. Be sure to include the statutory basis for doing so.

DO NOT TURN PAGE UNTIL COMPLETING THIS EXERCISE

Exercise Two

Kim and Chris are divorced and abide by a court-ordered time-sharing schedule. They have three children: Kylah, Corey, and Joshua, ages sixteen, twelve, and eight, respectively. The court-ordered time sharing schedule allows Chris to have every other weekend and alternating holidays with the children. Chris also has two months in the summer with the children.

Chris lives approximately four hours by car from Loveville, where the children live with Kim. Chris has been making the trip to Loveville regularly for three years. All three children are in public schools near the home they share with their mother. In addition, all participate in extra-curricular activities in the community. Kylah has started dating and Corey is playing championship soccer.

Both children love Chris, but feel that the time-sharing schedule is interfering with their social life and having a negative impact on their ability to focus on school work. Kim and Chris agree that the time-sharing schedule should be modified to better meet the children's needs.

Kim and Chris have come to see you to request that you draft a motion to modify the time-sharing schedule. They are both in complete agreement on the new terms of the time-sharing schedule. Has there been a substantial change in circumstances that would necessitate a new agreement? Is a substantial change in circumstances necessary, if both parties agree? Advise them of their rights.

Are you able to represent both parties, if they are in agreement? If so, draft the motion for them.

DO NOT TURN PAGE UNTIL COMPLETING THIS EXERCISE

Chapter Resources

RELEVANT STATUTE(S)

§ 61, Fla. Stat. (2013).

FORMS
Many of the forms you will need to practice family law in Florida can be accessed on the internet at:

http://www.flcourts.org/gen_public/family/forms_rules/index.shtml#900

FLORIDA FAMILY LAW RULES OF PROCEDURES

http://www.floridabar.org/TFB/TFBResources.nsf/Attachments/416879C4A88CBF04852 56B29004BFAF8/$FILE/311%20Family%20Law.pdf?OpenElement

A major part of your task is to select the correct form(s) to assist you in completing the Exercises.

CASES

1. *Lane v. Lane*, 16 So. 3d 179 (Fla. 5th DCA 2009).
2. *Washington v. Stevens*, 969 So. 2d 487 (Fla. 5th DCA 2007).
3. *Cheverie v. Cheverie*, 898 So. 2d 1028 (Fla. 5th DCA 2005).
4. *Vinnik v. Vinnik,* 831 So. 2d 1271 (Fla. 4th DCA 2002).
5. *Kazmierazak v. Query*, 736 So. 2d 106 (Fla. 4th DCA 1999).

Chapter Checklist

Did you ask or consider the following questions?

1. What are the names, ages, and birth dates of the minor children of the marriage?

2. Has a final judgment or recent order been entered by the court?

3. Has there been a substantial change in circumstances since the entry of the final judgment or most recent order?

4. Have any of the children reached the age of majority?

5. Have the parents created a parenting plan or entered into an informal time-sharing/support agreement?

6. With whom do the children currently reside?

7. Have the children expressed a preference for which parent they wish to reside with on a permanent basis?

8. Does either parent suffer from mental illness or an addiction?

9. Where do the parties currently reside?

10. Does either parent plan to move out of state or more than 50 miles from their current residence?

11. Does either party pay for health insurance or child care for the minor children?

12. Does the parent understand what is meant by equal time-sharing?

13. Does the parent understand what is meant by sole parental responsibility?

14. Should a guardian ad-litem be hired or appointment by the court?

SELF ASSESSMENT REFLECTION

WHAT I LIKED BEST ABOUT THE EXERCISE:

WHAT I LIKED LEAST ABOUT THE EXERCISE:

WHAT I LEARNED FROM THE EXERCISE:

SKILLS I HAVE ACQUIRED AFTER COMPLETING THE EXERCISE:

MY NOTES

APPENDIX

RESOURCES FOR STUDENTS AND ATTORNEYS

Resources for Students and Attorneys

❖ **Laws and Rules**

- Phyllis Coleman, *Florida Family Law Text and Commentary 2012 Statutes* (2013).
    - ◆ A collection of laws including the Florida Constitution, state and federal statutes affecting family law. Updated annually.

- *Florida Family Law Case Summaries* (8th ed. 2012).
    - ◆ A comprehensive review of Florida family case law organized into 9 topical chapters

- *Florida Family Law Handbook* (15th ed. 2009).
    - ◆ A collection of Florida statutes, federal statutes, and international treaties affecting family law.

- *Florida Family Law Set (Rules and Statutes)* (2013).
    - ◆ A comprehensive collection of Florida rules and state and federal statutes affecting family law, including Florida Family Law Rules of Procedure, Florida Rules of Civil Procedure, Florida Family Law Rules of Procedure Forms and Instructions, Florida Supreme Court Approved Family Law Forms and Instructions, and Florida Rules of Judicial Administration. Updated annually.

- *West's Florida Family Laws and Rules, 2013 ed.* (2013).
    - ◆ Florida family law statutes, Florida Rules of Juvenile Procedure and Florida Family Law Rules of Procedure and Forms.

    - ◆ Florida Rules of Court: Federal, State, and Local (2013). *Florida Rules of Court – State, Federal, and Local 2013 Revised ed. (Vols. I-III Florida Court Rules)* (2013).

    - ◆ A three-volume collection of all rules that affect cases in Florida. State Rules includes all Florida rules of procedure, including Rules of Family Court with Forms, Commentary, and Instruction. Also includes Rules of Juvenile Procedure, Rules for Court-Appointed Arbitrators, and Rules for Certified and Court-Appointed Mediators. Federal Rules includes all federal rules of procedure. Local Rules includes state rules of court administration for individual circuits that have published these rules. Updated annually.

❖ **Practice Materials**
❖ *General*
  ▪ *Florida Jurisprudence, Second Series* (2014).
    ◆ A modern comprehensive text statement of Florida law completely revised and rewritten in the light of modern authorities and developments.

  ▪ *Florida Jurisprudence Forms, Legal & Business* (1990).
    ◆ Includes forms for all areas of Florida law, including family law. Updated annually.

  ▪ Henry P. Trawick, Jr., *Trawick's Florida Practice and Procedure, 2012-2013 ed.* (2012).
    ◆ Trawick's Florida Practice and Procedure provides clear analysis of the state procedural rules, and their application in specific circumstances, including a chapter on family law.

  ▪ Brenda M. Abrams, *Florida Family Law* (1986).
    ◆ This comprehensive and current coverage of every aspect of Florida family law combines in-depth discussion with practice guides, forms and consultant Brenda Abrams' own analysis of marriage-related agreements and sample forms. Updated biannually.

  ▪ Gerald D. Schackow et al., *Florida Family Law Practice Manual* (1976).
    ◆ Treatise on marriage and child custody law in Florida, covering substantive and procedural law. Updated biannually.

❖ *Adoption*

  ▪ Florida Bar, Adoption, Paternity, and Other Florida Family Practice (10th ed. 2013). Carin M. Porras et al., *Adoption, Paternity and Other Florida Family Practice* (10th ed. 2012).
    ◆ This manual guides the practitioner through less familiar areas of family law.

  ▪ Melissa Tartaglia, *Adoption and Surrogacy in Florida: The Legal and Practical Sourcebook for Laypersons and Lawyers* (2011).
    ◆ Covers rights, responsibilities, and procedure.

❖ *Guardianship*

- David Brennan, *Florida Guardianship Law and Procedure* (2d ed. 2013).
  - ◆ Discusses the applicable Florida Statutes, Probate Court Rules, and local requirements that govern most of the proceedings and situations encountered by guardians and their counsel.

- *Florida Guardianship Practice* (7th ed. 2011).
  - ◆ Practice offers a concise, complete guide from pre-guardianship planning through termination. Explores guardianship alternatives, stressing medical and legal issues analyzing all facets of practice under F.S. Chapter 744.

❖ *Marriage*

- *Divorce in Florida (Florida Bar's FasTrain* (4th ed. 2005).
  - ◆ This one-volume manual provides a guide through the steps of a relatively uncomplicated dissolution of marriage proceeding.

- Cindy A. Crawford et al., *Drafting Marriage Contracts in Florida* (10th ed. 2012).
  - ◆ Guides the practitioner through drafting premarital or martial settlement agreements.

- *Enforcement of Final Judgments of Dissolution of Marriage* (3d ed. 2009)
  - ◆ Although the order granting dissolution of marriage is titled a final judgment, some aspects of the order are not final. The judgment may contain a provision retaining jurisdiction for enforcement and modification. Even without such a provision, however, the court retains jurisdiction for these purposes. Especially in dissolutions involving minor children, a party is likely to seek modification of the final judgment at some future date. Guides the practitioner through the process of modifying a final judgment. Practice pointers alert the reader to various procedural pitfalls and ethical issues. Forms are provided for all procedures discussed.

- *Florida Dissolution of Marriage* (11th ed. 2012).
    - ◆ Details the dissolution process from initial client interview through temporary relief and discovery to final judgment. Provides forms and checklists, including client questionnaires, pleadings, interrogatories, and provisions for final judgments and settlement agreements.

- *Florida Proceedings After Dissolution of Marriage* (11th ed. 2012).
    - ◆ Examines appeals, enforcement, and modification and addresses registration, enforcement, and modification of foreign judgments in Florida, the Child Support Enforcement Program, and the Uniform Interstate Family Support Act.

- Florida Bar, Matrimonial ADR – Mediation, Arbitration and Collaborative Lawyering (2002*). Matrimonial ADR – Mediation, Arbitration and Collaborative Lawyering* (2002).
    - ◆ Contains materials from a Continuing Legal Education seminar presented by the Florida Bar Family Law Section.